WORD POWER *for* GERMANS

3

TYPISCH DEUTSCHE
ENGLISCHFEHLER
UND IHRE VERMEIDUNG

Kunze / Woxbrandt / Rowden

BEAVER BOOKS

Die Deutsche Bibliothek - CIP-Einheitsaufnahme

Woxbrandt, Barbro:
Wordpower for Germans : "typisch deutsche" Englisch-Fehler und ihre Vermeidung / Woxbrandt/Kunze/Rowden. - Frankfurt am Main : Beaver Books.

Hauptbd.
3 . – (2000)
ISBN 3 - 926686 - 30 - 8

BEAVER BOOKS, Marburger Str. 15, 60487 Frankfurt/Main
Tel. 069/774047 • Fax 069/704635 • www.beaverbooks.de

WORDPOWER *for* GERMANS · 3

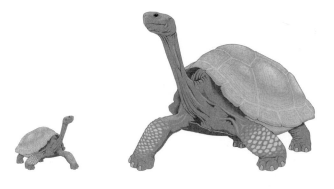

*Always remember, you'll never get anywhere
without sticking your neck out.*

C O N T E N T S

C O N T E N T S

$\mathcal{E}$NGLISH IDIOMS FOR GERMAN LEARNERS · 1

WORDPOWER ROCKETS

Form words with the letters from the rockets. You can use each letter as many times as you wish.
3 Letters = 1 Point;   4 Letters = 2 Points;   5 Letters = 3 Points;   6 Letters = 4 Points;   More = 5 Points;   All: 12 Points

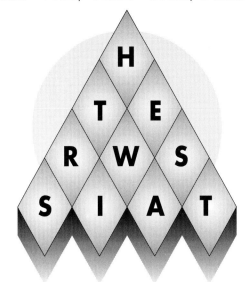

3 Letters _____

_____

_____

_____

4 Letters _____

_____

_____

_____

_____

5 Letters _____

_____

_____

6 Letters _____

More _____

All Letters: An English word that has entered the German language

W

3 Letters _____

_____

_____

_____

4 Letters _____

_____

_____

_____

_____

5 Letters _____

_____

_____

6 Letters _____

More _____

All Letters: A German word that has entered the English language

T

POINTS: **10** Take-off • **20** Try more boosters • **30** Gaining height • **40** In Orbit • **50** Stratosphere • **60** Planet Genius!

Important anniversaries are often celebrated with pathetic speeches.

FALSE FRIENDS 𝒞AN BE PATHETIC

There are many words in English that seem like welcome friends because they look the same (or nearly the same) as a German word. You cannot rely on this, however, because they quite often mean something completely different and lead you into making mistakes and talking nonsense. They are therefore also called **FALSE FRIENDS**.

Each of the sentences below contains one false friend; underline it and put it into the False Friend prison on the opposite page; then choose the correct word from the grey box and add it to the end of each line.

dedicated • delicious • fantastic • final • foreign • graceful • highly-gifted • lazy

lively • masterful • sensitive • **solemn** • solid • sprightly • stuffy • wretched

1. Important anniversaries are often celebrated with pathetic speeches. _____   **solemn** _____

2. This table is made of massive oak. _____   _____

3. Edward could be a good student if he wasn't so foul. _____   _____

4. The air in the waiting room was hot and sticky. _____   _____

5. We listened to a virtuous interpretation of Ravel's 'Bolero'. _____   _____

6. Be careful when you talk to Mimosa, she's very sensible. _____   _____

7. My grandparents are both over 80, but they're still very vital. _____   _____

8. What our country needs is more outlandish investment. _____   _____

9. My uncle doesn't like people, but he's a genial scientist. _____   _____

10. Thank you so much for your dinner invitation, the meal was costly. _____   _____

11. The ballerina delighted the audience with her gracious dance steps. _____   _____

12. The third goal made Liverpool's defeat perfect. _____   _____

13. The Albanian economy is still in a desolate state. _____ _____

14. The teachers at our school are all very engaged. _____ _____

15. Not many people know him, but he's a famous comic. _____ _____

16. Melanie is very temperamental and always in good spirits. _____ _____

FALSE FRIENDS PRISON

	pathetic							

Now release the false friends by using them with their correct meaning to complete the sentences below.

1. The Eiffel Tower is one of Europe's most _____ landmarks.

2. The Queen is widely admired for the _____ way she talks to ordinary people.

3. The footballer was sent off the pitch for _____ play.

4. In the hot car the box of chocolates had turned into a _____ mess.

5. I would hate to live on a _____ island miles from any form of civilization.

6. These tiles are _____ for our new bathroom.

7. Immediate medical help is of _____ importance after a heart attack.

8. In the Valley of the Kings the Egyptians built temples on a _____ scale.

9. With her friendly and _____ approach to guests Ann has made her hotel a great success.

10. We had to give up our plans to extend the kitchen as the whole project would be too _____ .

11. Our boss is very _____ – one wrong word and he flies into a rage.

12. During the recent famine in Ethiopia the poor starving children made a _____ sight.

13. Nuns and priests take a vow that binds them to a _____ life style.

14. Sarah and Ben seem the ideal couple and have recently become _____ to marry.

15. Be _____ ! Think! You can't go to a business lunch in a T-shirt.

16. John arrived at the funeral in a red suit, really his dress sense is quite _____ !

7

NO APPLAUSE FOR THE Circus ARTIST

Some false friends are lurking among the compounds and expressions below. Find them and be immune to them forever, then write down the correct forms by choosing from the real friends in the grey box.

area	brochure	dressing	handle	lens	**performer**	slogan	tag
bench	budget	flake	haven	package	raid	strainer	varnish
box	campaign	floss	instructor	pad	range	stroke	watch

advertising action _____

air attack _____

ballot urn _____

breast swimming _____

camera objective _____

circus artist _____**circus performer**_____

dental silk _____

door grip _____

election parole _____

grey zone _____

household deficit _____

nail lack _____

park bank _____

price etiquette _____

product palette _____

salad sauce _____

skiing teacher _____

snow flock _____

tax oasis _____

tax packet _____

tea sieve _____

travel prospect _____

wrist clock _____

writing block _____

1. Unsere Werbeaktion war ein großer Erfolg.

2. Der Journalist hatte seinen Schreibblock vergessen.

3. Die Wahlparole unserer Partei ist „Weniger Steuern".

4. Das neue Steuerpaket senkt das Haushaltsdefizit.

5. Wir müssen den Türgriff auswechseln.

6. Ich habe einen sehr guten Skilehrer.

7. Wir haben unsere Produktpalette erweitert.

8. Die Isle of Man ist eine Steueroase.

9. Dieser Reiseprospekt enthält einige gute Angebote.

10. Die Nato flog Luftangriffe gegen Serbien.

11. Die Wahlurne ist ein Symbol für die Demokratie.

12. Handgefertigte Armbanduhren sind sehr teuer.

13. Mein Zahnarzt empfiehlt die Verwendung von Zahnseide.

14. Sanft fielen Schneeflocken vom Himmel.

15. Sie saß auf einer Parkbank und fütterte die Vögel.

16. Nagellack ist meistens rot.

17. Die Frage der Bankgebühren ist eine Grauzone.

18. Ich entfernte das Preisetikett von Rays Geschenk.

My husband is a real cavalier of the old school

WHEN *C*AVALIERS ARE FALSE FRIENDS

Write down the real friends of the words below by choosing from the grey boxes.

audience	**parliamentary party**	Anstreicher, Maler	Kreis
bonus payment	reading /reading matter	Aussicht	Öffentlichkeit
tin, can	slogan	Dosis	Vorlesung, Vortrag
brochure	suitcase	Genugtuung	Truhe
compasses	department	Urlaubsort	**Bruchteil**
restaurant / inn	window dresser	Hafturlaub	Pension

≠

ENGLISH	← GERMAN • ENGLISH →	GERMAN
parliamentary party =	Fraktion ≠ fraction =	**Bruchteil**
_____ =	Gasthaus ≠ guest house =	_____
_____ =	Dose ≠ dose =	_____
_____ =	Dekorateur ≠ decorator =	_____
_____ =	Gratifikation ≠ gratification =	_____
_____ =	Ressort ≠ resort =	_____
_____ =	Koffer ≠ coffer =	_____
_____ =	Lektüre ≠ lecture =	_____
_____ =	Parole ≠ parole =	_____
_____ =	Prospekt ≠ prospect =	_____
_____ =	Publikum ≠ public =	_____
_____ =	Zirkel ≠ circle =	_____

USE THE ENGLISH EXPRESSIONS FROM THE OPPOSITE PAGE TO COMPLETE THE SENTENCES.

1. A good _____ can make a Christmas store window look magical.

2. Because of his good behaviour the prisoner was allowed out of jail on _____ .

3. Brighton is a famous English seaside _____ .

4. Buckingham Palace is now open to the _____ each summer.

5. If you want to draw an exact _____ you need _____ .

6. I have brought plenty of _____ to keep me occupied on the long journey.

7. I was pleased to leave my heavy _____ at the airline's check-in counter.

8. I will collect some travel _____ so that we can choose a holiday.

9. I'm afraid we cannot deal with your enquiry here, you need the finance _____ .

10. I didn't hesitate for a _____ of a second when they made me that fantastic offer.

11. It's not possible to increase social benefits as the state _____ are empty.

12. We didn't like the food at our _____ so we went to a _____ .

13. "Meat means murder" is a _____ used by vegetarian activists.

14. Pete took a _____ of Coke and opened the biscuit _____ .

15. The _____ applauded loudly at the end of the concert.

16. The _____ said it would take a week to finish painting the house.

17. The doctor prescribed a _____ of medicine three times a day.

18. The _____ of a good job leads many students to study hard.

19. The students found their professor's _____ interesting and enlightening.

20. The workers were promised a _____ if they completed the work a month early.

21. Anne's parents were filled with _____ when they saw their daughter's diploma.

nocturnal animal = _____   facial expression = _____   federal authority = _____

WORD FORMATION

Im Deutschen werden Komposita (compounds) oft aus zwei Substantiven zusammengefügt: **Atom + Kraft = Atomkraft, Medizin + Student = Medizinstudent**. Von dieser Technik der Wortbildung macht auch das Englische auf ganz ähnliche Weise Gebrauch: **Tageslicht – day light, Wassersport – water sports, Arbeitsmoral – work ethic**.

Zu beachten ist aber, dass viele solcher Zusammensetzungen im Englischen durch andere Kombinationen wiedergegeben werden: **Arbeitsbedingungen – working conditions, Arbeitsbereich – field/area of work, Arbeitskampf – industrial dispute / industrial action**. Diese werden auf den folgenden Seiten vorgestellt.

Beginnen Sie mit der Kombination Adjektiv+Substantiv und bilden Sie die folgenden Zusammensetzungen:

aquiline	federal	hereditary	native		area	designer	engineering	punishment
basic	foreign	**industrial**	natural	**+**	authority	disaster	knowledge	speaker
capital	genetic	interior	residential		biologist	disease	minister	warming
environmental	global	marine	toxic		damage	**dispute**	nose	waste

Adlernase _____

Arbeitskampf _____ **industrial dispute** _____

Außenminister _____

Bundesbehörde _____

Erbkrankheit _____

Erderwärmung _____

Gentechnologie _____

Giftmüll _____

Grundkenntnisse _____

Innenarchitekt _____

Meeresbiologe _____

Muttersprachler _____

Naturkatastrophe _____

Todesstrafe _____

Umweltschäden _____

Wohngebiet _____

solar eclipse

solar system

solar energy

sunburn

FIND THE ODD ONE OUT

Find the odd one out and write the German translation underneath each word.

1. Solar ○ eclipse ○ system ○ energy ○ **burn**

2. Annual ○ accounts ○ salary ○ book ○ general meeting

3. Dental ○ brush ○ surgery ○ treatment ○ floss

4. Marital ○ status ○ vow ○ bliss ○ row

5. Nuclear ○ test ○ submarine ○ scientist ○ bomb

6. Lunar ○ landing ○ landscape ○ light ○ eclipse

7. Mortal ○ danger ○ enemy ○ penalty ○ sin

8. Commercial ○ fair ○ law ○ traveller ○ school

9. Small ○ car ○ finger ○ child ○ change

10. Criminal ○ prevention ○ law ○ offence ○ record

13

watering can

parking meter

magnifying glass

GERUND COMPOUNDS

Form compounds by pairing up the elements in the grey box.

advertising	filling	reading	stumbling		agency	ground	**pad**	star
cleaning	**launching**	shooting	swimming		block	hours	plaster	station
dialling	magnifying	sparking	talking		boy	lady	plug	streak
driving	opening	spelling	whipping		code	meter	point	test
dumping	parking	sticking	winning		glass	mistake	room	trunks

Abschussrampe _____ **launching pad** _____

Badehose _____

Führerscheinprüfung _____

Gesprächsthema _____

Glückssträhne _____

Heftpflaster _____

Lesesaal _____

Lupe _____

Müllkippe _____

Öffnungszeiten _____

Parkuhr _____

Prügelknabe _____

Rechtschreibfehler _____

Reinemachefrau _____

Sternschnuppe _____

Stolperstein _____

Tankstelle _____

Vorwahl _____

Werbeagentur _____

Zündkerze _____

MORE GERUND COMPOUNDS

Gerund Compounds bestehen – genau wie deutsche Substantivzusammensetzungen – aus einem Grundwort und einem Bestimmungswort, welches das Grundwort hinsichtlich seiner Art oder Funktion näher definiert.

Da die deutschen Entsprechungen vieler Gerund Compounds ebenfalls durch eine Kombination aus Verbalsubstantiv + Substantiv (z.B. Schlaftablette) ausgedrückt werden, hat das Direktübersetzungsteufelchen (nach dem Muster: Schlaf = sleep, Tablette = pill, Schlaftablette ≠ sleep pill) oft leichtes Spiel (richtig: **sleeping pill**).

Beachten Sie bei der Aussprache, dass Gerund Compounds den sogenannten **compound stress** tragen, der eine echte Wortzusammensetzung von Ausdrücken unterscheidet, die keine eigene Bedeutungseinheit darstellen:

a black **bi**rd = ein schwarzer Vogel (kein compound); a **black**bird = eine Amsel (compound, neue Einheit)

a singing **tea**cher = ein singender Lehrer; a **sing**ing teacher = ein Gesangslehrer

a sleeping **child** = ein schlafendes Kind; a **slee**ping pill= eine Schlaftablette

CHOOSE THE CORRECT NOUN TO COMPLETE THE GERUND COMPOUNDS BELOW

Aktenschrank	**filing** .... ○ cupboard	✗ cabinet	○ desk
Bademantel, Morgenrock	dressing .... ○ gown	○ coat	○ skirt
Brutstätte	breeding .... ○ place	○ ground	○ local
Eislauf-, Rollschuhbahn	skating .... ○ slope	○ hall	○ rink
Essgewohnheiten	eating .... ○ habits	○ customs	○ traditions
Fahrlehrer	driving .... ○ teacher	○ instructor	○ assistant
Fischereihafen	fishing .... ○ haven	○ city	○ port
Operationssaal	operating .... ○ sale	○ theatre	○ hall
Schlafsack	sleeping .... ○ bag	○ sack	○ bed
Verkaufsargument	selling .... ○ argument	○ reason	○ point
Verkaufsautomat	vending .... ○ machine	○ automat	○ gadget
Wahllokal	polling .... ○ station	○ local	○ room
Wanderung	walking .... ○ journey	○ trip	○ tour
Wettbüro	betting .... ○ office	○ shop	○ bureau
Zeltplatz	camping .... ○ place	○ site	○ space

bird of prey

coat of arms

work of art

YOUR BAPTISM OF FIRE

Form compounds by pairing up the elements in the grey box.

baptism	chamber	house	reign		cards	face	nerves	representatives
beast	date	kiss	state	*of*	commerce	**fire**	paradise	speech
bird	figure	loss	talk		contract	honour	prey	terror
breach	guest	means	theory		delivery	life	proof	the town
burden	house	presence	war		emergency	mind	relativity	transport

Beweislast _____

Ehrengast _____

Feuertaufe _____ **baptism of fire** _____

Fortbewegungsmittel _____

Geistesgegenwart _____

Gesichtsverlust _____

Handelskammer _____

Kartenhaus _____

Lieferdatum _____

Mund-zu-Mund-Beatmung _____

Nervenkrieg _____

Notstand _____

Paradiesvogel _____

Raubtier _____

Redewendung _____

Relativitätstheorie _____

Repräsentantenhaus (USA) _____

Schreckensherrschaft _____

Stadtgespräch _____

Vertragsbruch _____

OF COMPOUNDS

Pair up the elements in the grey box by combining them with 'of' and complete the sentences below.

bed	country	freedom	shadow		birth	heart	love	roses
bird	creature	holy	standard	*of*	doubt	holies	mind	speech
breach	date	labour	state		**grandeur**	law	origin	strength
change	**delusions**	rule	tower		habit	living	prey	the peace

1. Pride goes before a fall – _____**delusions of grandeur**_____ often result in people's downfall.

2. The American Bald Eagle is perhaps the world's most impressive _____.

3. _____ is important for democracy. We must all be able to say what we think.

4. I don't expect any money from writing my father's biography, it's purely a _____.

5. Man is a _____ . Once you've settled into a routine it's hard to start something new.

6. You have to work hard to get ahead, life is not a _____ , you know.

7. My uncle has helped us so much in our time of crisis; he really is a _____.

8. There can be no stable society without a proper respect for the _____.

9. To the community of Wagner fans the Bayreuth festival is the _____.

10. The accident was a great shock and people are still in a very confused _____.

11. According to EC rules all meat products must carry a label identifying the _____.

12. What's your _____ ? – I was born on July 8th, 1976.

13. I think this man is innocent without a _____.

14. At first Mr May wouldn't allow his daughter to marry Jim, but then he had a _____.

15. Wealth isn't everything. A high _____ is no guarantee for happiness.

16. Three football hooligans were arrested for a _____.

at your service

a holiday at the seaside

shouting at each other

PREPOSITIONS AT YOUR $ERVICE

DEUTSCH: ANDERE PRÄPOSITION ➜ ENGLISCH: **AT**

Die folgende Übersicht erhebt keinen Anspruch auf Vollständigkeit, sondern konzentriert sich auf deutsch-englische Unterschiede, die beim Gebrauch der Präpositionen erfahrungsgemäß zu Stolpersteinen und Fehlerquellen werden.

jem. anstarren / anschreien	stare / shout at somebody
sich etwas anschauen	to look at something
einen Stein nach jem. werfen	throw a stone at somebody
auf jem. (etwas) zeigen	point at someone (sth)
vor nichts zurückschrecken	stop at nothing
über jemanden/etwas lachen	laugh at someone/something
an etwas reissen	tear at something
nach jemandem schlagen	strike at somebody
auf etwas schießen (zielen)	shoot (aim) at something
auf etwas zeigen	point at something
an die Decke schauen	look up at the ceiling
mit Gewinn/Verlust verkaufen	sell sth at a profit/loss
s. an einen Strohhalm klammern	clutch (grasp) at straws
auf einer Party / Beerdigung	at a party / funeral
auf einer Hochzeit / Auktion	at a wedding / at an auction
auf eigene Kosten	at one's own expense
auf eigenes Risiko	at one's own risk
Es steht viel auf dem Spiel	There is a lot at stake
Wir stehen an deiner Seite	We're at your side
auf hohem Niveau	at a high level
Er raucht nie bei der Arbeit	He never smokes at work
an einem Tisch sitzen	sit at a table
Es ist jemand an der Tür	There's someone at the door
zu einem hohen Preis	at a high price
um jeden Preis	at any price
zum gleichen Preis	at the same price

Liebe auf den ersten Blick	love at first sight
am Steuer	at the steering wheel
„am Ruder"	at the helm
bei uns zuhause	at our place (in our home)
an der Grenze	at the border
Napoleons Niederlage bei W.	Napoleon's defeat at Waterloo
am Meer	at the seaside
Hält dieser Zug in Rye?	Does this train stop at Rye?
an der Bonner Universität	at Bonn university
bei der geringsten Berührung	at the slightest touch
bei voller Geschwindigkeit	at full speed
beim ersten Anblick	at first sight
beim Anblick von Blut	at the sight of blood
beim ersten Versuch	at the first attempt
an / auf / bei der Arbeit	at work
hart bei der Arbeit sein	be hard at work
bei der Geburt	at birth
nach eigenem Gutdünken	at one's own discretion
jem. im Schach schlagen	beat someone at chess
in regelmäßigen Abständen	at regular intervals
im Vorteil / Nachteil	at an advantage/a disadvantage
in „aller Ruhe"	at leisure
im rechten Winkel zu	at a right angle to
am Bahnhof / am Flughafen	at the station / at the airport
gut (schlecht) in Mathematik	good (bad) at mathematics
im Grunde	at bottom

am Anfang des Jahrhunderts ..... at the beginning of the century		im richtigen/letzten Moment ..... at the right/last moment
bei Sonnenaufgang .... at dawn (sunrise)		im Schneckentempo .... at a snail's pace
bei Sonnenuntergang .... at sundown (sunset)		zu jener Zeit .... at that time
Schau mich an! .... Look at me!		jmdm. zu Diensten stehen .... be at someone's service
nachts .... at night		zur Verfügung stehen .... be at someone's disposal
um Mitternacht .... at midnight		in einem frühen Stadium .... at an early stage
Er deutete es an .... He hinted at it		bei der ersten Gelegenheit .... at the first opportunity
Um wieviel Uhr? .... At what time?		in der Schule / im Büro .... at school / at the office
im Alter von vier Jahren .... at the age of four		in einer Höhe / Tiefe von .... at a height / depth of
beim Frühstück (Dinner) .... at breakfast (dinner)		auf dem Höhepunkt der Krise ... at the height of the crisis
im Moment .... at present (at the moment)		bei einer Temperatur von .... at a temperature of

TRANSLATE THE SENTENCES BY USING PREPOSITIONAL PHRASES WITH <u>AT</u>

1. Der Strand steht unseren Gästen zur Verfügung. _____

2. Es war Liebe auf den ersten Blick. _____

3. Das Experiment ist in einem frühen Stadium. _____

4. Ich habe im Moment keine Zeit. _____

5. Ich werde Tom bei der ersten Gelegenheit fragen. _____

6. Rose ist in der Schule, ihre Mutter ist im Büro. _____

7. Das Wrack liegt in einer Tiefe von 50 Fuß. _____

8. Wasser kocht bei einer Temperatur von 100 Grad. _____

9. Der Unfall geschah bei hoher Geschwindigkeit. _____

10. Ich traf Susan auf einer Party. _____

11. Eric will diesen Vertrag um jeden Preis. _____

12. Zu jener Zeit war Finnland ein Teil Schwedens. _____

13. Das Schiff liegt in der Bucht vor Anker. _____

14. Wir verbringen unsere Ferien immer am Meer. _____

15. Maria war immer schon gut in Englisch. _____

16. Dieser Zug hält nicht in Ashford. _____

17. Manche Leute schrecken vor nichts zurück. _____

18. Alle lachten über Kims Witze. _____

19

*Will all those who are <u>not</u> **in favour** of my proposal please raise their hands and say 'I resign'.*

JOIN THE *in*-CROWD

DEUTSCH: ANDERE PRÄPOSITION → ENGLISCH: **IN**

Folgende Darstellung konzentriert sich auf Fälle, in denen das Englische die Präposition **in** gebraucht, das Deutsche hingegen eine andere. Die Vielzahl der Fälle, in denen das Deutsche und Englische im Gebrauch dieser Präposition übereinstimmen, sei deshalb hier nur erwähnt. Auf eine Angabe von „Regeln" wurde bewusst verzichtet, da diese stets nur einige wenige Fälle abdecken könnten. Bitte beachten Sie, dass Sie sich stets den präpositionalen Ausdruck in seiner Gesamtheit als eigene Vokabel einprägen sollten.

meiner Meinung nach	in my opinion (view)
ein Ansteigen der Preise	a rise (an increase) in prices
am Morgen / Abend	in the morning / evening
am Nachmittag	in the afternoon
auf Englisch schreiben	write in English
einer von 10	one in ten (one out of ten)
für ewige Zeiten	in perpetuity
vor den Augen aller	in full view of everybody
eine Wolke am Himmel	a cloud in the sky
sich für etwas interessieren	be interested in
das Interesse an etw. verlieren	lose interest in something
Vertrauen haben zu	have faith / confidence in
Schwierigkeit haben mit	have difficulty in
für etwas sein	be in favour of something
an etwas teilnehmen	take part in
Erfolg haben mit	succeed in
Mitspracherecht haben bei	have a say (voice) in sth
Zuflucht bei etwas suchen	take refuge in
bei einem Unfall umkommen	be killed in an accident
vor meinem geistigen Auge	in my mind's eye
mit Textilien handeln	deal in textiles
den Kopf vor Scham senken	hang one's head in shame
Das Kind schrie vor Schreck	The child screamed in terror
auf dem Marktplatz	in the market place

auf der Suche nach	in search (in quest) of
Schmerzen haben	be in pain
auf der Durchreise	in transit
auf Lager	in stock
auf dem Lande	in the country
auf die Dauer	in the long run
auf einem Foto (Bild)	in a photo (picture)
bei gutem Wetter	in good weather
aller Wahrscheinlichkeit nach	in all probability / likelihood
gut bei Kasse sein	be in cash / be in funds
an der Macht sein	be in power
auf dem Rückzug sein	be in retreat
bei guter Laune sein	be in a good mood
Tom ist bei der Polizei	Tom's in the police
arm an / reich an	poor in / rich in
mit lauter Stimme	in a loud voice
auf diese Weise	in this way
bei guter Gesundheit	in good health
zu Ehren von	in honour of
zum Gedenken an	in memory of
schwarz auf weiß	in black and white
blind auf einem Auge	blind in one eye
an etwas glauben	believe in something
sich jmdm. anvertrauen	confide in someone

rich in Vitamin C

in good health

in a hurry

COMPLETE THE SENTENCES BY USING PREPOSITIONAL PHRASES WITH IN

1. You can hear our teacher in the next classroom because he always speaks _____ .

2. Why are you so aggressive? You'll never get anywhere if you treat people _____ .

3. It took me a while to recover from my operation, but now I am _____ again.

4. A siesta is a short sleep or rest people in hot countries have _____ .

5. The state dinner at Windsor Castle was held _____ the American president.

6. We had wonderful weather in Spain, there was not a cloud _____ .

7. I spent all afternoon in the shops _____ a good pair of shoes.

8. I know you all think that John is strange, but _____ he is quite a nice man.

9. According to the opinion polls the Republicans _____ will lose the election.

10. I'm sorry, I'm American and don't speak your language. Can you say it _____ ?

11. Mr May insists on a written contract. He wants to have everything _____ .

12. Most people love the summer, there is so much more you can do _____ .

13. I hate big cities, I would much rather live _____ in some small village.

14. When I got my camera, my nephews came running as they wanted to be _____ .

15. A commemoration service was held _____ the war victims.

16. Lemons are _____ Vitamin C which helps you keep _____ .

17. Tom was _____ , he was laughing and smiling and gave us all a big hug.

18. James Dean was killed _____ while driving his new sports car.

21

over the piano

across the piano

at the piano

on piano

BRUSH UP *Y*OUR PREPOSITIONS · 1

Warum ist der Musiker '**on** piano' aber steht das sangesfrohe Feiertrio '**at** the piano'? Bitte fragen Sie uns nicht, denn die englischen Präpositionen (Verhältniswörter) entziehen sich meist logischen Erklärungen. In sich selbst oft recht bedeutungsarm, sind Präpositionen meist in feststehende Redewendungen eingebunden. Es ist deshalb sinnvoll, stets den gesamten Ausdruck als eigene Vokabel zu lernen.

Die folgenden Übersetzungsübungen konzentrieren sich auf Fälle, bei denen erfahrungsgemäß häufig Verwechslungen auftreten. Die korrekten englischen Präpositionen sehen Sie jeweils am rechten Rand der Zeile.

AN

1. Komm und setz' dich **an** meine Seite. **(by)**

   Come and sit by my side.

2. Darf ich dich **an** dein Versprechen erinnern? **(of)**

3. Ich denke oft **an** die schöne Zeit in Rom. **(of)**

4. Die Kinder nahmen sich **an** der Hand. **(by)**

5. In 1867 verkaufte Russland Alaska **an** Amerika. **(to)**

6. Schrei' mich nicht so **an**. **(at)**

7. Gregory erinnert mich **an** einen alten Schulfreund. **(of)**

22

AUS

1. Was ist **aus** ihm geworden? **(of)**

2. **Aus** welchem Grunde hast du das getan? **(for)**

3. Ich habe **aus** Versehen den Computer ausgeschaltet. **(by)**

4. Dieser Tisch ist **aus** Holz. (Ausgangsmaterial erkennbar) **(of)**

5. Öl wird **aus** Oliven gemacht. (Ausgangsmaterial nicht mehr erkennbar) **(from)**

BEI

1. Sue wohnt noch **bei** ihren Eltern. **(with)**

2. Besuche **bei** Alan sind immer interessant. **(to)**

3. Ich will mich **bei** Ihnen entschuldigen / beschweren. **(to)**

4. Es gelang uns **beim** ersten Versuch. **(at)**

5. Morgan ist jetzt 20 Jahre **bei** der Firma. (Present Perfect) **(with)**

BIS

1. Ich muss den Essay **bis** (spätestens) morgen fertig haben. **(by)**

2. Wir können (die ganze Zeit) **bis** Mai hier bleiben. **(until)**

3. Ich habe das Buch (nur) **bis** Seite 30 gelesen. **(up to)**

4. Kinder **bis** sechs Jahre haben freien Eintritt. **(up to)**

into the water   *in the water*

IN ► INTO

Der Gebrauch der englischen Präposition **in** stimmt in weiten Bereichen mit dem Deutschen überein; allerdings sollte man sich deshalb nicht in Sicherheit wiegen, denn viele Ausdrücke erfordern die Präposition **into**, die Veränderung, Übergang, Bewegung (in etwas hinein) betont.

1. Ich möchte dieses Geld **in** Dollar umtauschen. **(into)**

2. Emma brach **in** Tränen aus. **(into)**

3. Wir arbeiten oft bis weit **in** die Nacht. **(into)**

4. Unser Cousin will **in** die Politik gehen. **(into)**

5. Hitler stürzte (to plunge) Europa **in** einen fürchterlichen Krieg. **(into)**

6. Fährst du heute nachmittag **in** die Stadt? **(into)**

7. Samantha übersetzte den Brief **ins** Englische. **(into)**

IN / IM

1. Wir wohnen **im** dritten Stock. **(on)**

2. Hast du das Fußballspiel **im** Fernsehen gesehen? **(on)**

3. Tardy macht alles immer **in** der letzten Minute. **(at)**

4. Mein Onkel heiratete **im** Alter von 60 Jahren. **(at)**

MIT

1. Kommst du **mit** dem Zug oder **mit** dem Auto? **(by)**

2. Kann ich **mit** Scheck bezahlen? **(by)**

3. Er kommt **mit** dem nächsten Flugzeug / Bus / Zug. **(on)**

4. Der Kunde beschwerte sich **mit** lauter Stimme. **(in)**

5. Kim ist seit drei Jahren **mit** Al verheiratet. **(to)**

NACH

1. In Köln können Sie **nach** Düsseldorf umsteigen. **(for)**

2. Wir alle sehnen uns **nach** dem Frühling. **(for)**

3. Tipsy riecht immer **nach** Bier. **(of)**

4. Mr Grubber strebt **nach** Geld und Einfluss. **(for)**

ZWISCHEN

1. Ich saß **zwischen** John und Ingrid. **(between)**

2. Ich saß **zwischen** meinen vielen Verwandten. **(among)**

3. Das Kaufhaus ist **zwischen** zwei und vier geschlossen. **(between)**

4. Die Katze lag **zwischen** den Blumen. **(among)**

5. Hannover liegt **zwischen** Frankfurt und Hamburg. **(between)**

SAME WORD – DIFFERENT PREPOSITIONS

Einige Verben und Adjektive gehen Verbindungen mit verschiedenen Präpositionen ein, was häufig zu Verwechslungen führt.

arrive at Kleinere Orte (Örtlichkeiten), Bahnhöfe, Flughäfen
*The train arrived **at** Paddington half an hour late. – I arrived **at** Salisbury, hired a car and drove on. – We arrived **at** Heathrow / **at** Victoria Station.*

arrive in Länder, größere Städte, Inseln sowie Orte (Örtlichkeiten), die für den Ankommenden wichtig oder von persönlichem Interesse sind ► *The President arrived **in** Washington. – I arrived **in** my hometown where my family was waiting for me.*
* Siehe Infokasten zu at/in auf dieser Seite

ask for bitten um ► *The immigration officer asked **for** our passports.*

ask after sich nach jemandem erkundigen ► *Aunt Mary asked **after** Rebecca.*

ask about sich nach etwas erkundigen ► *I'll ask the station manager **about** the train times.*

compare with vergleichen mit (gleichartigen Dingen) ► *You can't compare London **with** Berlin, they are too different. – Compared **with** Poland, Germany has a high standard of living.*

compare to im übertragenen Sinn gleichstellen mit andersartigen Dingen ► *Parks are often compared **to** the lungs of a city. – Shall I compare thee **to** a summer's day? (Shakespeare)*

consist of bestehen aus ► *Water consists **of** hydrogen and oxygen.*

consist in bestehen in ► *The secret of happiness consists **in** always being optimistic. – My job consists **in** preparing the briefs for Mr Harris.*

deal with handeln von; sich mit etwas befassen; mit jmdm. umgehen
*These books deal **with** British history. – An ambulance team always has to deal **with** the injured first. – Mr Stroppy is very difficult to deal **with**.*

deal in handeln mit; Handel treiben mit
*A stockbroker deals **in** shares. – My uncle deals **in** electrical goods.*

DEUTSCH: IN → ENGLISCH: AT

Bei Bezug auf Gebäude oder Örtlichkeiten, in oder an denen etwas geschieht, verwendet das Englische **at**, wenn die Funktion des Ortes im Mittelpunkt des Interesses steht und die räumliche Ausdehnung als solche von keinem oder geringem Interesse ist.

Er arbeitet im British Museum. / Er raucht nie im Büro.	He works **at** the British Museum. / He never smokes **at** the office.
Ich wohne in der Kennedystr. 24 (genau Adresse)	I live **at** 24, Kennedy Road.
aber: Ich wohne in der Kennedystraße.	I live in Kennedy Road.
in der Schule/der Kirche (beim Unterricht / Gottesdienst)	**at** school / **at** church
in der Schule/der Kirche (im Schulgebäude / in der Kirche)	in the school / in the church
Der Zug hält nicht in Rye; wir steigen in Lyme um.	The train doesn't stop **at** Rye, we'll change **at** Lyme.
ein Konzert in der Albert Hall / der Film im Empire-Kino	a concert **at** the Albert Hall / the movie **at** the Empire cinema
die Ausstellung in der Tate Gallery	the exhibition **at** the Tate Gallery

Alternativ kann in vielen Fällen ohne größeren Bedeutungsunterschied auch **in** verwendet werden, wenn eher das Sich-befinden innerhalb eines Raumes / einer Räumlichkeit betont werden soll: A state dinner **at** Buckingham Palace / A state dinner **in** Buckingham Palace. – Let's meet **at** the cinema. / Let's meet **in** the cinema.

distinguish between	unterscheiden zwischen ▸ *A child must learn to distinguish **between** right and wrong.*	
distinguish from	unterscheiden von ▸ *You can distinguish a camel **from** a dromedary by its two humps.*	

---

die of/from — sterben an (innere Ursache)
*Soon after he retired, he died **of** a heart attack. – My uncle died **from** lung cancer.*

die by — sterben durch (äußere Einwirkung) ▸ *He who lives by the sword, shall die **by** the sword.*

die in — bei etwas sterben ▸ *Five people died **in** an accident on the M2.*

---

discriminate between — unterscheiden / einen Unterschied machen
*People who are colour-blind are unable to discriminate **between** certain colours.*

discriminate against — jemanden diskriminieren ▸ *America has laws that make it illegal to discriminate **against** minorities. – Foreigners are discriminated **against** in many European countries.*

---

hear of — etwas hören / erfahren über jemanden ▸ *Have you heard **of** this wonderful new actor?*

hear from — hören / Nachricht erhalten von jemandem ▸ *Have you heard anything **from** Gerald?*

---

look after — sich um etwas kümmern ▸ *Can you look **after** the baby while I'm out?*

look for — etwas suchen ▸ *Al is looking **for** a new job. – I'm looking **for** my keys, have you seen them?*

look at — etwas ansehen / betrachten ▸ *I looked **at** the wonderful painting. – Look **at** me.*

---

shout to — jemandem (etwas) zurufen ▸ *'Hello Mike, nice to see you,' she shouted **to** me.*

shout at — jemanden anschreien ▸ *'Get out of my garden,' the man shouted **at** us.*

---

think of — an etwas / jemanden denken
*We often think **of** our holiday on Barbados. – I can't think **of** anything but you, darling.*

think about — über etwas nachdenken, überlegen ▸ *Have you ever thought **about** the future?*

---

be angry about — böse / ärgerlich auf eine Sache ▸ *The travellers were very angry **about** the delay.*

be angry with — böse / ärgerlich auf eine Person ▸ *The teacher was very angry **with** Adrian.*

---

anxious about — besorgt sein um jemanden / etwas ▸ *We were rather anxious **about** Tim.*

anxious for — begierig auf / auf etwas aus sein ▸ *Diana was anxious **for** a good result in her exam.*

---

critical of — kritisch gegenüber jemandem / etwas ▸ *Sue was very critical **of** her husband's behaviour.*

critical to — entscheidend für ▸ *This contract is critical **to** the survival of our firm.*

---

made of — Ausgangsmaterial unmittelbar erkennbar
*This door is made **of** steel, this pot is made **of** clay, this desk is made **of** wood.*

made from — Ausgangsmaterial im Endprodukt nicht mehr direkt erkennbar
*Wine is made **from** grapes, beer is made **from** hops, yoghurt is made **from** milk, petrol is made **from** oil, paper is made **from** wood.*

TRANSLATING THE UNTRANSLATABLE · 1

*S*prache ist niemals nur die Mitteilung von Sachverhalten, sondern stets auch lebendiger Dialog mit emotionalen Untertönen. Eine wichtige Rolle kommt deshalb den sogenannten Modalpartikeln zu, die als „Würzwörter", „Abtönungswörter" oder „Mittel der Satzbelebung" den Äußerungen eine bestimmte (subjektive) Tönung geben und dadurch eventuellen Missverständnissen vorbeugen, indem sie die innere Einstellung des Sprechers – also z.B. Zustimmung, Ablehnung, Einschränkung, Erstaunen, Interesse – signalisieren und verdeutlichen.

In sich selber bedeutungsarm sind diese Partikeln meist in idiomatische Redewendungen eingebunden und lassen sich deshalb auch nicht direkt „übersetzen". Oft hat das Englische auch eine völlig neue idiomatische Entsprechung für dieselbe Situation und die entsprechende Kommunikationsabsicht. Am besten erschließt sich dieser Bereich des Spracherwerbs deshalb, indem man sich möglichst viele Beispiele einprägt.

ABER

Der Kaffee ist **aber** heiß.	Oh, this coffee is hot.
Das ging **aber** schnell.	That was quick.
Das war **aber** Pech.	That really was bad luck.
Dann ist er **aber** wütend geworden.	And then he really got mad. / Did he go mad!
Das geht jetzt **aber** zu weit.	That's really going too far, now.
Kann ich Sie etwas fragen? – **Aber** ja.	Can I ask you something? – Yes, of course you can.
Bist du **aber** schlau.	Aren't you clever!

BLOSS

Hätte er **bloß** auf mich gehört.	If only he had listened to me.
Was ist **bloß** los mit dir?	What is the matter with you?
Wer hat dir das **bloß** erzählt?	Whoever told you that?
Tu das **bloß** nicht wieder.	Don't you dare do that again.
Warum hast du das **bloß** getan?	Now, why did you do that?

AUCH

Warum muss er **auch** so viel trinken?	Well, why does he have to drink so much?
Er nahm die Zeitung, ohne **auch** nur zu fragen.	He took the newspaper without even asking.
Auch Ärzte können sich irren.	Even doctors can be wrong, you know.
Hast du **auch** deine Zähne geputzt?	You've brushed your teeth, haven't you? You did brush your teeth, didn't you?
Tim fährt einen Ferrari. – Er hat ja **auch** viel Geld.	Tim drives a Ferrari. – Well, he's got a lot of money. Tim drives a Ferrari. – He's got a lot of money, after all.
Wie dem **auch** sei . . .	Be that as it may . . .
Auch wenn er noch so viel verdient . . .	However much he earns / may earn . . .
Hast du **auch** alles verstanden?	Did you understand everything okay? You did understand everything, didn't you?

DENN

Was willst du **denn** machen?	What are you going to do, then?
Was ist **denn** mit dir passiert?	What happened to you, then?
Wie soll ich das **denn** wissen?	How should I know?
Hast du **denn** keinen Hunger?	Aren't you hungry, then?
Was soll das **denn**?	What do you think you're doing?
Wie läuft's **denn** so?	How is it going, then?

DOCH

(Ach,) Hör **doch** auf.	Oh, stop it, for heaven's sake. / Oh, stop it, will you.
Sei **doch** nicht traurig.	Don't be sad.
Lass mich **doch** in Ruhe.	Leave me alone, will you.
Das ist **doch** kein Problem!	That's no problem, really.
Rufen Sie mich **doch** morgen früh an.	Why don't you give me a ring tomorrow morning?
Frag' **doch** deinen Lehrer.	Why don't you ask your teacher?
Wie war sein Name **doch** gleich?	What was his name again?
Komm' **doch** einfach mal vorbei.	Why don't you drop in some day? / Just drop in some day.
Frag' **doch** mal Tom.	Why don't you ask Tom?
Du willst **doch** sicher mit Mary sprechen.	You want to talk to Mary, don't you?
Ich liebe dich. Das weißt du **doch**.	I love you. You know that, don't you?
Er wollte eigentlich nicht, aber er kommt **doch**.	He didn't want to come, but now he's coming after all.
Und sie (die Erde) bewegt sich **doch**. (Galilei)	And it does move.
Du trinkst wohl keinen Wein, Sean. – **Doch**!	You don't drink wine, do you? – As a matter of fact, I do.

EBEN

Dann müssen wir **eben** zu Hause bleiben. .... Well, we'll just have to stay at home, then.

Das ist es ja **eben**. .... Well, that's exactly what I mean. / That is the point.

Ich habe mich **eben** geirrt. Na und? .... So I was wrong. So what?

So ist das **eben**. .... Well, that's the way it is.

Eben das meine ich. .... That's exactly what I mean.

Eben deshalb. .... That is exactly why.

EIGENTLICH

Bist du **eigentlich** oft in London? .... Tell me, do you go to London often?

Wie spät ist es **eigentlich**? .... What's the time, by the way?

Also **eigentlich** hab ich keine Lust. .... Well, actually I don't feel like it.

Eigentlich dürfen wir hier nicht rein. .... Strictly speaking, we're not allowed in here.
We shouldn't really be in here.

Ray ist **eigentlich** ganz nett. .... Ray's quite nice, really.

Eigentlich würde ich lieber zu Hause bleiben. .... I'd rather stay at home, to be honest.
Well, to be honest, I'd rather stay at home.

Was machst du **eigentlich** hier? .... What are you doing here, anyway?

ERST

Wir kommen **erst** sehr spät in Malaga an. .... We won't get to Malaga until very late.

Ich bin **erst** seit einer Stunde hier. .... I've only been here for an hour.

Warum sagst du mir das **erst** jetzt? .... Why didn't you tell me this before?

Wenn du das **erst** einmal hinter dir hast . . . . Once you've got that behind you . . .

So etwas sollte gar nicht **erst** passieren. .... These things shouldn't happen in the first place.

Was wird dann **erst** passieren? .... Whatever will happen then?

ETWA

Glaubt er mir **etwa** nicht? .... Doesn't he believe me?

Hältst du mich **etwa** für blöd? .... You don't think I'm stupid, do you? / I'm not stupid, you know.

Glaubst du das **etwa**? .... You don't believe that, do you?

Sie kommen doch, oder **etwa** nicht? .... You'll be coming, won't you? / You're coming, aren't you?

Hast du **etwa** schon wieder verschlafen? .... Don't tell me you've overslept again.

Wollen Sie **etwa** schon gehen? .... Surely you are not leaving already?

Er ist nicht **etwa** dumm, sondern nur faul. .... It's not that he is stupid, just lazy.

REVISION: TRANSLATION

1. Kann ich hier rauchen? – Aber ja.

2. Du kennst doch sicher Herrn Swift?

3. Ich habe eben mal einen Fehler gemacht. Na und?

4. Komm doch mal vorbei.

5. Will Edna etwa nicht mit uns kommen?

6. Ich trinke eigentlich keinen Wein, aber ein Glas nehme ich doch.

7. Hast du auch alles gepackt?

8. Warum bist du eigentlich nach Brighton gezogen?

9. Ist der letzte Bus weg? Dann müssen wir eben laufen.

10. Wie willst du denn nach London kommen?

11. Wären wir bloß vorsichtiger gewesen.

12. Rede bloß nicht noch einmal so mit mir.

13. Auch Lehrer können die Geduld verlieren.

14. Du erwartest doch nicht etwa, dass ich das glaube.

on top of the world

*Who says that
you can't teach
an old dog new tricks?*

*giving someone
the cold shoulder*

on cloud number nine

letting off steam

*We'll bend over backwards
to give you good service*

*sweeping something
under the carpet*

*like a bear
with a sore head*

*I'm sick and tired
of working with you,
Griswald. I RESIGN!*

drinking like a fish

*An apple a day
keeps the doctor away*

*Don't bury your
head in the sand*

Silence is golden

*I'll keep my fingers
crossed for you*

Time flies

ENGLISH IDIOMS
FOR GERMAN LEARNERS

*V*okabel- und Grammatikkenntnisse sind zwar das unabdingbare Gerüst einer Sprache, aber eben nur das Gerüst. So richtig spannend und reizvoll wird der Fremdsprachenerwerb erst auf der Stufe der Idiomatik: der Welt jener typischen Redewendungen und Ausdrucksformen, die in bildhafter und prägnanter Form bestimmte Sachverhalte und menschliche Reaktionsweisen, Gemütszustände und Handlungen auf den Punkt bringen. Sie hauchen der sprachlichen Kommunikation Leben und Farbe ein, machen das Gesagte erlebbar und nachvollziehbar, originell und lebendig und geben Ihren Äußerungen einen unverwechselbaren persönlichen Charakter.

Sprachliche Äußerungen ohne jegliche idiomatische Wendungen werden im Englischen sehr schnell als flach und fade empfunden. Nur mit diesem „Salz in der Suppe" erhalten Gespräche mit Engländern und Amerikanern die persönliche und vertraute Note, welche die Voraussetzung für eine ungezwungene Unterhaltung ist. Der lebendige Gebrauch idiomatischer Formen ist dabei keineswegs auf den Bereich des persönlichen Gesprächs begrenzt, sondern erstreckt sich über die gesamte Bandbreite der sprachlichen Ausdrucksformen.

Aus dem großen Reichtum idiomatischer Wendungen des Englischen präsentieren die folgenden Übungen und Darstellungen solche Idioms, die eine – mehr oder weniger direkte – Entsprechung im Deutschen haben, da diese einerseits besonders gut zugänglich und einprägsam sind, andererseits aber auch wegen der typischen deutsch-englischen Fallen besonders zu Bewusstsein gebracht werden müssen.

Ein ausführliches **Register** der präsentierten Idioms finden Sie im Key ab Seite 43.

MOUNTAINS & MOLEHILLS

Wo Deutsche aus einer Mücke einen Elefanten machen, verwandeln englische Muttersprachler einen Maulwurfshügel in einen Berg. Beide meinen dasselbe: übertreiben, etwas aufbauschen. Wie in diesem Falle gibt es im Deutschen und Englischen zahlreiche Entsprechungen bei Redewendungen, die im Kern dasselbe ausdrücken, sich aber in der Wahl des bildhaften Ausdrucks unterscheiden.

Den ersten Teil der englischen Ausdrücke finden Sie jeweils im oberen, den zweiten Teil im unteren grauen Kasten.

ado	apples	birds	bolt	carrot	cart	finger	**mountain**
rhyme	root	side	slap	sledgehammer	tip	virtue	voice

blue	branch	coin	face	horse	**molehill**	necessity	nothing
nut	oranges	pie	reason	stick	stone	tongue	wilderness

| aus einer Mücke einen Elefanten machen | ▶ | make a **mountain** out of a **molehill** |
| die Stimme des Rufers in der Wüste | | |

aus einer Mücke einen Elefanten machen ▶ make a **mountain** out of a **molehill**

Es liegt mir auf der Zunge ▶ It's on the _____ of my _____

aus der Not eine Tugend machen ▶ make a _____ of _____

Zuckerbrot und Peitsche ▶ the _____ and the _____

ohne Sinn und Verstand ▶ without _____ or _____

ein Blitz aus heiterem Himmel ▶ a _____ from the _____

mit Kanonen auf Spatzen schießen ▶ use a _____ to crack a _____

die Stimme des Rufers in der Wüste ▶ a _____ crying in the _____

Äpfel mit Birnen vergleichen	►	compare	_____	with	_____
Die Kehrseite der Medaille	►	the other	_____	of the	_____
zwei Fliegen mit einer Klappe schlagen	►	kill two	_____	with one	_____
ein Schlag ins Gesicht	►	a	_____	in the	_____
Viel Lärm um Nichts	►	Much	_____	about	_____
das Pferd beim Schwanz aufzäumen	►	put the	_____	before the	_____
eine Hand (mit) im Spiel haben	►	have a	_____	in the	_____
an Haupt und Gliedern reformieren	►	reform something	_____	and	_____

OFFICE WISDOM

Das Englische liebt Wortspiele, in denen die übertragen-bildhafte Eigenlogik des idiomatischen Ausdrucks und die Ebene der wörtlichen Bedeutung seiner Komponenten spielerisch ineinander übergehen. Das Spektrum reicht hierbei von – wenig geistreichen – 'school boy jokes' bis zu geschliffenen politischen oder philosophischen Aperçus. Besonders viele solcher Wortspiele sind durch die Büro- und Arbeitswelt inspiriert. Hier einige Kostproben:

Unless you are an elevator operator you can't get ahead simply by running people down.

A chip on the shoulder is often a piece of wood that has fallen from the head.

It takes more than a shoeshine to give someone polish.

Taking the line of least resistance often makes people and rivers crooked.

If success turns your head, you'll probably end up moving in the wrong direction.

Just because you are paranoid doesn't mean they are not out to get you.

Reputation is a large bubble which bursts when you try to blow it up yourself.

A friend is someone who says nice things about you behind your back.

Someone should tell him the difference between pulling his weight and throwing it around.

*My husband and I are cutting down on Christmas presents
this year. A new Jacuzzi for little Fido here and a couple of luxury cars,
diamond rings and mink coats for our fifty closest friends, but that's where we **draw the line**.*

DRAWING THE LINE

Verb+Noun Idioms: Choose the correct NOUN to complete the idiom that corresponds to the German expression.

German				
Grenzen setzen	▶ **draw**	○ the limit	○ **the line**	○ the border
die Arbeit niederlegen	▶ down	○ work	○ tools	○ the job
den Bach runtergehen	▶ go down	○ the drain	○ the stream	○ the river
in die Brüche gehen	▶ go	○ in breaks	○ into pieces	○ to pieces
sein wahres Gesicht zeigen	▶ show one's true	○ colours	○ face	○ soul
das Kriegsbeil begraben	▶ bury	○ the war axe	○ the hatchet	○ the war hatchet
jmdn. bis ins Mark treffen	▶ shake someone	○ in the heart	○ to the core	○ in the mark
seinen Meister finden	▶ meet one's	○ winner	○ master	○ match
Partei ergreifen	▶ take	○ party	○ sides	○ preference
in Rätseln sprechen	▶ talk in	○ puzzles	○ riddles	○ enigmas
aus dem Ruder laufen	▶ get out of	○ hand	○ rudder	○ sight

den Schein aufrecht erhalten	▶	keep up	○ appearances	○ the shine	○ the appearance
den Schwung verlieren	▶	run out of	○ swing	○ speed	○ steam
die Stellung halten	▶	hold	○ the position	○ the fort	○ the standing
in Verbindung bleiben	▶	keep in	○ connection	○ touch	○ line
nicht mit der Wimper zucken	▶	not bat	○ an eyelid	○ an eyelash	○ an eyebrow

NOW USE THE IDIOMS TO COMPLETE THE FOLLOWING SENTENCES

1. I don't mind the odd erotic scene in a movie, but I _____**draw the line**_____ at full frontal nudity.

2. Manchester United seemed invincible this season, but with Liverpool they've _____ .

3. Please promise to _____ . I'd like to know how you are getting on.

4. He always says he's generous but he _____ when he refused to lend me money.

5. At first the demonstration was peaceful, but when the police arrived the situation _____ .

6. I thought he'd be shocked when I told him I would leave him, but he _____ .

7. I'm sorry, I don't know what you are talking about. You _____ .

8. Some people who lose their job _____ by pretending to go to work each morning.

9. The money we had invested in the company _____ when they went bankrupt.

10. Sue and Ray have always been quarrelling, but now their relationship has really _____ .

11. The employees decided to _____ when they heard of the new working conditions.

12. You'll have to settle this argument among yourselves. Don't expect me to _____ .

13. My sister and I hadn't spoken for a year but we _____ when our mother was ill.

14. It's always the same with Tim. He starts new projects but after a week he _____ .

15. I have to leave the office for an hour. Can you _____ for me?

16. It _____ when Ellen, whom I had trusted most, turned against me.

37

LEAVE NO STONE UNTURNED!

Something went wrong with the idioms below. Pair them up correctly, then write them next to their German equivalents.

add _____	one's belt
call _____	like a chimney
clutch _____	someone the moon
go _____	something at face value
keep _____	a hornet's nest
leave **no stone unturned**	someone to the skies
let _____	a spade a spade
overshoot _____	at straws
praise _____	fuel to the fire / to the flames
promise _____	someone on their toes
smoke _____	like clockwork
stir up _____	the mark
take _____	someone stew in their own juice
tighten _____	**no stone unturned**

jemandem goldene Berge versprechen ► _____

die Dinge beim Namen nennen ► _____

den Gürtel enger schnallen ► _____

etwas für bare Münze nehmen ► _____

Öl ins Feuer gießen ► _____

jemanden im eigenen Saft schmoren lassen ► _____

rauchen wie ein Schlot ▶ _____

wie am Schnürchen gehen / laufen ▶ _____

sich an jeden Strohhalm klammern ▶ _____

jemanden in den höchsten Tönen loben ▶ _____

jemanden auf Trab halten ▶ _____

nichts unversucht lassen ▶ _____

in ein Wespennest stechen ▶ _____

über das Ziel hinaus schießen ▶ _____

COMPLETE THE SENTENCES BELOW BY ADDING THE APPROPRIATE IDIOMS

1. You can't go on spending more than you earn! You'll have to _____ .

2. Although the doctor has told him to give up cigarettes, Brian _____ .

3. Anne's desserts are immensely popular and our dinner guests always _____ .

4. I love gardening, it gives me something to do and it _____ .

5. The police have promised to _____ in order to find the missing child.

6. Don't yell back at people who scream at you in traffic, it only _____ .

7. In a liberal society the police should not _____ when fighting crime.

8. The opposition decided to do nothing and let the government _____ .

9. Mark is very straightforward and outspoken, he always _____ .

10. Don't _____ everything he says at _____ , he's often quite ironic.

11. I hate the way some banks _____ with their investment schemes.

12. The newspaper _____ with their investigation into police corruption.

13. We experienced none of the difficulties we had expected, it all _____ .

14. We know we _____ but this operation is our last chance to save our child.

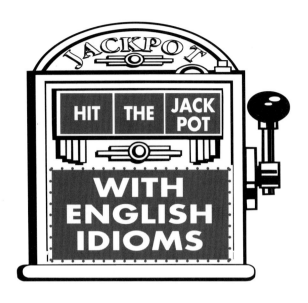

HIT THE IDIOM JACKPOT

VERB+NOUN Idioms: You'll find the VERBS in the upper and the NOUNS in the lower grey box.

bark	**hit**	lift	pick	stick
call	keep	nip	rap	strike
close	leave	pay	settle	throw

balance	deal	**jackpot**	lurch	score
bone	finger	knuckles	pace	tree
bud	guns	lip-service	ranks	tune

das große Los ziehen ► _____**hit**_____ the _____**jackpot**_____

keinen Finger rühren ► not _____ a _____

jmdm. auf die Finger klopfen ► _____ someone over the _____

aus dem Gleichgewicht bringen ► _____ off _____

handelseinig werden ► _____ a _____

sich auf dem Holzweg befinden ► _____ up the wrong _____

mit jem. ein Hühnchen zu rupfen haben ► have a _____ to _____ with someone

etwas im Keim ersticken ► _____ something in the _____

Lippenbekenntnisse ablegen ► _____ _____ (to sth)

eine (alte) Rechnung begleichen ► _____ an (old) _____

die Reihen schließen ► _____ _____

Schritt halten (mit) ► _____ _____ (with sb/sth)

auf seinem Standpunkt beharren ► _____ to one's _____

jemanden im Stich lassen ► _____ someone in the _____

den Ton angeben ► _____ the _____

NOW USE THE IDIOMS TO COMPLETE THE FOLLOWING SENTENCES

1. I love my new job. I've got wonderful colleagues and a good salary. I've really _____ .

2. Politicians _____ to the need for human rights but do nothing to really protect them.

3. In World War I Britain promised the Arabs a country of their own, but then shamefully _____ .

4. Will food production be able to _____ with the ever-growing world population?

5. Neo-nazi movements are dangerous, and society must _____ before they can spread.

6. Many westerns tell the story of a lone gunman coming into a town to take revenge and _____ .

7. Some people call Al stubborn, but I admire the way he always _____ .

8. There won't be peace in Northern Ireland until all sides _____ and stick to it.

9. When the opposition attacks a minister it's the cabinet's duty to _____ .

10. With some football clubs the manager doesn't have a say any longer. It's the players who _____ .

11. Mr Sawyer is a strong and unemotional man and it is not easy to _____ .

12. The police think the terrorist is still in town, but I think they _____ .

13. Come here, young man, I have _____ . Was it you who ate all the biscuits?

14. Don't expect me to help you after all you've done to me. I _____ to help you.

15. It is the Supreme Court's job to _____ the government _____ if they act against the constitution.

STOP TWIDDLING YOUR THUMBS

Verb+Noun Idioms: Choose the correct VERB to complete the idiom that corresponds to the German expression.

German				English
Däumchen drehen	○ turn	○ **twiddle**	○ rotate	**one's thumbs**
einen neuen Anfang machen	○ make over	○ turn over	○ make	a new leaf
Berge versetzen	○ change	○ replace	○ move	mountains
ein Eigentor schießen	○ score	○ shoot	○ strike	an own goal
sich glücklich schätzen (können)	○ estimate	○ calculate	○ count	oneself lucky
unter den Hammer kommen	○ arrive	○ become	○ go	under the hammer
das Gehirn zermartern	○ rack	○ torture	○ martyr	one's brains
mit Glacéhandschuhen anfassen	○ finger	○ handle	○ touch	with kid gloves
aus der Luft greifen (erfinden)	○ pluck	○ grip	○ take	something from the air
jemandem im Nacken sitzen	○ breathe down	○ sit in	○ sit on	someone's neck
die Nase über jem./etwas rümpfen	○ wrinkle	○ rump	○ turn up	your nose at sb/sth
die Ohren spitzen	○ sharpen	○ prick up	○ erect	one's ears
aufs falsche Pferd setzen	○ back	○ set on	○ sit on	the wrong horse

jemandem in den Rücken fallen	○ fall .... ○ attack .... ○ stab	someone in the back
etwas in den Schatten stellen	○ move .... ○ stand .... ○ put	something in the shade
das Schicksal herausfordern	○ challenge .... ○ try .... ○ tempt	fate / providence
den Weg ebnen	○ pave .... ○ level .... ○ even	the way
die Zähne zusammenbeißen	○ compress .... ○ grit .... ○ bite	one's teeth

NOW USE THE IDIOMS TO COMPLETE THE FOLLOWING SENTENCES

1. Please let me help you, I can't just sit here and _____ .

2. In what has been called the auction of the century this painting will _____ today.

3. Our new product is the best on the market. It _____ everything else _____ .

4. Good mountain climbers avoid all unnecessary risks, they never _____ .

5. Governments _____ by raising taxes as this means less investment.

6. John is very sensitive, you have to _____ , or he is immediately upset.

7. I've got to finish the sales presentation by tomorrow. My boss is already _____ .

8. Jo's been in prison twice, but now he's married and has _____ .

9. The country's first free elections _____ for a democratic future.

10. The US have often _____ in dealing with South American governments.

11. Don't_____ at people less intelligent than you – they too have their qualities.

12. When I heard my name mentioned I _____ with interest.

13. I've been _____ all afternoon, but I can't remember his telephone number.

14. Believe in yourself and you can achieve anything; you know what they say – faith can _____ .

15. Stop complaining about the boss. You can _____ that he didn't sack you.

16. I know we are all tired, but we'll just have to _____ and finish the job in time.

17. I must warn you of Phil. He acts friendly to your face, but in the end he will _____ .

18. You just can't take Tom's theories seriously, he just _____ his arguments _____ .

I'll scratch your back if you'll scratch mine. How about it?

AS THE SAYING GOES

Im Deutschen und Englischen gibt es zahlreiche Entsprechungen bei Redewendungen, die sich in der Wahl des bildhaften Ausdrucks unterscheiden aber im Kern dasselbe ausdrücken.

Führen Sie die vorgegebenen deutschen Ausdrücke mit ihren englischen Entsprechungen (grauer Kasten) zusammen.

Eine Hand wäscht die andere   **I'll scratch your back, if you scratch mine.**

Aus den Augen, aus dem Sinn   _____

Ich verstehe nur Bahnhof   _____

Kümmere dich nicht um ungelegte Eier   _____

Ich fresse einen Besen, wenn . . .   _____

Die Dummen werden nicht alle   _____

Das dicke Ende kommt noch   _____

ins Fettnäpfchen treten   _____

Dem Fuchs sind die Trauben zu sauer   _____

Das ist gehupft wie gesprungen   _____

sich nicht in die Karten schauen lassen   _____

Kopf hoch! _____

gute Miene zum bösen Spiel machen _____

Über Geschmack lässt sich nicht streiten _____

jemandem / etwas aus dem Weg gehen _____

Dreimal darfst du raten _____

der Tropfen, der das Fass zum Überlaufen bringt _____

Wenn alle Stricke reißen . . . _____

Morgen ist auch noch ein Tag _____

etwas Tür und Tor öffnen _____

sich übernehmen _____

Davon geht die Welt nicht unter _____

AS THE SAYING GOES . . . WIE MAN SO SCHÖN SAGT

△ **I'll scratch your back, if you scratch mine.**

△ when the worst comes to the worst

△ This is not the end of the world

△ bite off more than one can chew

△ I'll eat my hat, if . . .

△ the straw that breaks the camel's back

△ I'll give you three guesses

△ out of sight, out of mind

△ open the floodgates to something

△ put one's foot in it

△ It's sour grapes. / Sour grapes

△ Keep your chin up! / Chin up!

△ put a brave face on something

△ play one's cards close to one's chest

△ There's a sucker born every minute

△ There's no accounting for tastes.

△ steer clear of someone / something

△ It's all Greek to me

△ There's a sting in the tail

△ Cross that bridge when you come to it

△ That's six of one and half a dozen of the other

△ Tomorrow is another day

45

BRIGHT SPARKS

Viele idiomatische Adjektiv+Substantiv-Kombinationen des Deutschen haben eine Entsprechung im Englischen, die sich allerdings nicht über eine Direktübersetzung erschließen lässt.

Wählen Sie die korrekten Ausdrücke und verwenden Sie sie zur Vervollständigung der Sätze auf der gegenüberliegenden Seite.

mit bloßem Auge	○ with the mere eye	○ **with the naked eye**	○ with the only eye
mit angehaltenem Atem	○ with held breath	○ with suspended breath	○ with bated breath
ein unbeschriebenes Blatt	○ an empty quantity	○ an unknown quantity	○ an unwritten leaf
ein schwaches Bild	○ a poor show	○ a weak picture	○ a weak show
wie ein geölter Blitz	○ like oiled lightning	○ like greased lightning	○ like oiled thunder
böses Blut	○ evil blood	○ wicked blood	○ bad blood
ein heißes Eisen	○ a hot potato	○ a hot iron	○ a warm iron
ein böses Erwachen	○ a rude awakening	○ a bad awakening	○ an evil awakening
das schöne Geschlecht	○ the beautiful sex	○ the pretty sex	○ the fair sex
dummes Geschwätz	○ stupid talking	○ idle talk	○ idiotic talk
einmalige Gelegenheit	○ golden opportunity	○ rare opportunity	○ one and only opportunity
mit bloßen Händen	○ with one's bare hands	○ with one's mere hands	○ with one's naked hands
ein alter Hase	○ an old hare	○ an old master	○ an old hand

ein wunder Punkt	○ a painful point	○ a sore point	○ a wounded point
eine Sackgasse	○ a blind alley	○ a sack alley	○ a blind way
ein hohes Tier	○ a big animal	○ a high animal	○ a big gun

USE THE ENGLISH EXPRESSIONS FROM THE OPPOSITE PAGE TO COMPLETE THE SENTENCES.

1. Mars is one of the planets which you can see with the _____ **naked eye** _____ .

2. Checking his bank account Roy had a _____ – there was hardly any money left.

3. The noise of Ray's lawn mower led to _____ between him and the neighbours.

4. We all watched the death-defying stunts of the tightrope walker _____ .

5. Ken has been with us for years, he's an _____ and knows everything about the business.

6. Trying to give state money to ailing industries is bound to fail, it's just another _____ .

7. Rescue workers arriving at the scene of the accident had to drag out injured people _____ .

8. When the police arrived the burglar was off _____ .

9. Incredible! They lost five-nil against this mediocre team – what a _____ !

10. I hear you've been offered a job in the City of London? Don't miss this _____ .

11. We know nothing about the form of the new tennis player – he is very much an _____ .

12. Don't mention his divorce to Sam, it is a bit of a _____ with him.

13. Do you know anything about the new chairman? I hear he is a _____ from America.

14. Women are sometimes called the _____ .

15. The question of whether or not to allow in more asylum seekers is a _____ in Germany.

16. They say the local factory is about to close, but there's no truth in that. It's just _____ .

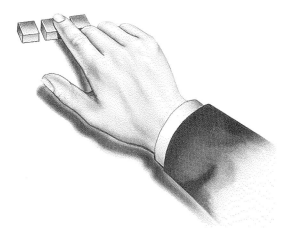

IDIOMS AT THE TOUCH OF A BUTTON

Kleine Ursache – große Wirkung. Wo im Deutschen und Englischen idiomatische Ausdrücke sowohl in der Wahl des bildhaften Ausdrucks wie der dafür verwendeten Elemente übereinstimmen, gilt es gleichwohl aufzupassen, wenn dabei Präpositionen mit im Spiel sind (**auf** Knopfdruck – **at** the touch of a button). Diese sind wesentliche Bestandteile des Gesamtausdrucks; und mit der Wahl der falschen Präpositionen löst sich unter Umständen die ganze Bedeutung des Ausdrucks auf. Auch hier steckt also der Teufel im Detail. Achten Sie dabei besonders auf die folgenden kleinen Präpositionsteufelchen.

Seite **an** Seite – side **by** side

auf Knopfdruck – **at** the touch of a button

auf Zeit spielen – play **for** time

in Frage stellen – call **into** question

in letzter Minute – **at** the last minute

über Bord gehen – go **by** the board

auf den ersten Blick – **at** first sight / glance

in die Knie zwingen – bring someone **to** their knees

vor die Hunde gehen – go **to** the dogs

ein Schuss **vor** den Bug – a (warning) shot **across** someone's bows

aus den Nähten platzen – burst **at** the seams

vom Sehen (her) kennen – know someone **by** sight

sich einen Namen machen – to make a name **for** oneself

vor Neid/Neugier platzen – burst **with** envy/curiosity

in die Geschichte eingehen – go **down in** history

sein Herz **an** etwas verlieren – lose one's heart **to** something

in Lachen/Tränen ausbrechen – burst **into** laughter/tears

die Nase **über** etwas rümpfen – turn up your nose **at** something

vom hohen Ross herunterkommen – come down **off** one's high horse

an einem (seidenen) Faden hängen – hang **by** a thread

jemandem etwas **ins** Gesicht sagen – say something **to** someone's face

der Schwanz wedelt **mit** dem Hund – the tail is wagging the dog

es steht ihm **ins** Gesicht geschrieben – it's written all **over** his face

vor jemandem/etwas den Hut ziehen – take one's hat off **to** someone/something

etwas **in** seinen Grundfesten erschüttern – shake the foundations of something

den Wald **vor** lauter Bäumen nicht sehen – not see the wood **for** the trees

48

TRANSLATION

1. Lass uns auf Zeit spielen. _____

2. Es war Liebe auf den ersten Blick. _____

3. Der Konzertsaal platzte aus allen Nähten. _____

4. Dieser Prozess war ein Schuss vor den Bug. _____

5. Warum kannst du mir das nicht ins Gesicht sagen? _____

6. Alle meine Freunde brachen in Lachen aus. _____

7. Ich ziehe den Hut vor Dianas Leistung. _____

8. Ich habe mein Herz an Sue verloren. _____

9. Komm' endlich von deinem hohen Ross runter. _____

10. Herr Burden kannte Betty vom Sehen. _____

11. Dieser Maler machte sich in Paris einen Namen. _____

12. Alle seine Prinzipien gingen über Bord. _____

13. Ohne neue Aufträge geht unsere Firma vor die Hunde. _____

14. Der Fall der Berliner Mauer ist in die Geschichte eingegangen. _____

15. Wir erreichten den Zug in letzter Minute. _____

16. Alle platzten vor Neugier, als Jamie zurück kam. _____

17. Der Skandal hat die Partei in ihren Grundfesten erschüttert. _____

18. Dieser Test stellt die Qualität des neuen Modells in Frage. _____

19. Nach der Operation hängt Ralfs Leben am einem seidenen Faden. _____

20. Die Rezession hat viele Firmen in die Knie gezwungen. _____

21. Du solltest nicht über andere Leute die Nase rümpfen. _____

22. Der Computer zeigt auf Knopfdruck die neuen Preise. _____

Is Mr Ironbender on the warpath again?

IDIOMS ON THE WARPATH

Use the idiomatic expressions from the grey box to complete the sentences below.

along the line	in high places	on the map	through thick and thin
at a low ebb	in the dark	on the right track	to the core
below the belt	off the hook	on the spur of the moment	**up for grabs**
from top to bottom	on common ground	out of the blue	up to scratch

1. This is an interesting competition with £ 50,000 in prizes _____ **up for grabs** _____

2. None of us had expected Harry, but then he suddenly turned up _____

3. I don't see how they could give Neil that job, he must have friends _____

4. 'East of Eden' was the film that made James Dean famous and put him _____

5. First his wife left him and then he lost his job. No wonder that Phil is mentally _____

6. We all know that Jimmy is not particularly bright, but to call him stupid was a blow _____

7. Nobody's perfect. We all make mistakes somewhere _____

8. My sister and I quarrel a lot, but with regard to our parents' happiness we are _____

9. I'm very sorry, but you make too many mistakes, your work is just not _____

10. The team of scientists celebrated because their experiments proved that they had been _____

11. A true football fan will support his team _____

12. We never plan our holidays. We just book something _____

13. Every spring we thoroughly clean our house _____

14. John was accused of theft, but his employer's alibi got him _____

15. I'm sorry, I don't have any information on this; I'm completely _____

16. I never thought Adrian had such right-wing views. I was shocked _____

MORE
OFFICE WISDOM

*They call him 'Jigsaw' because every time
he's confronted with a problem he goes to pieces.*

Pair up the following

The person who doesn't let the grass grow under his feet	until he sticks his neck out.
Ambition means working yourself to death	would be satisfied with even a small flame now.
The best way to convince a fool that he is wrong	is in clover.
Many a person who burned the candle at both ends	in order to live better.
I don't understand how rumours without a leg to stand on	is to let him have his own way.
Remember the turtle – he never makes any progress	can get around so fast.

51

PUT YOUR IDIOMS INTO PRACTICE

Viele idiomatische Ausdrücke stimmen im Deutschen und Englischen sowohl in der Wahl des bildhaften Ausdrucks wie der dafür verwendeten Elemente überein; gleichwohl gibt es feine Unterschiede, die zu beachten sind. So verwenden einige deutsche Idioms **einen bestimmten Artikel** (der, die, das), auf den der englische „Kollege" verzichtet.

FORM THE ENGLISH IDIOMS, THEN ADD THEM TO THEIR GERMAN EQUIVALENTS

be	bring	cast	get	go	keep	live	**play**	play	put	save	take

_____ up appearances   _____ from hand to mouth

_____ face   _____ something to heart

_____ second fiddle   _____ in seventh heaven

_____**play**_____ with fire   _____ to light

_____ into gear   _____ into practice

_____ down in history   _____ pearls before swine

mit dem Feuer spielen   **play with fire** _____

von der Hand in den Mund leben _____

sich etwas zu Herzen nehmen _____

in die Gänge kommen _____

die zweite Geige spielen _____

in die Geschichte eingehen _____

das Gesicht wahren _____

im siebten Himmel sein _____

ans Licht bringen _____

Perlen vor die Säue werfen _____

in die Praxis umsetzen _____

den Schein aufrecht erhalten _____

1. Carol has agreed to marry Graham and now he _____ .

2. If you are not prepared to _____ you should not accept the post of vice-president.

3. Don't _____ Ken's criticism _____ , he doesn't really mean what he says.

4. Whoever finds a cure for cancer will _____ .

5. Dictators like to _____ , but it's their people who get burnt in the end.

6. Teenagers will do anything to _____ in front of their peers.

7. The company tried to hush up the scandal, but a TV documentary _____ .

8. Come on, let's go, we must _____ , if we want to finish this job by next week.

9. He's an impoverished aristocrat, but still drives his Daimler to _____ .

10. Many people in third world countries don't have any property but just _____ .

11. The management are too stupid to take up his excellent ideas; he _____ .

12. I like your ideas, the only trouble is: will we be able to _____ them _____ ?

- **ein Wettlauf mit der Zeit – a race against time**
  When people have been buried by an avalanche any rescue operation is a race against time.

- **auf den ersten Blick – at first glance / at first sight**
  At first glance Mr May's office looks rather chaotic, but actually he's a very organised man.

- **wie ein geölter Blitz – like greased lightning**
  The children were off like greased lightning when they heard the ice cream van coming.

- **Dem Himmel sei Dank – thank heavens**
  Thank heavens Jane isn't coming, she would only have spoilt the party.

- **auf dem Papier – on paper**
  His theories look all right on paper, but they'll never work in the real world.

- **die Hölle auf Erden – hell on earth**
  Building the Panama Canal was hell on earth for the workers.

- **der Schwanz wedelt mit dem Hund – the tail is wagging the dog**
  A smaller coalition party mustn't be seen to determine government policy – it would be a case of the tail wagging the dog.

Please believe me, Johnson, I would never say such a thing
to your face; I only ever said it behind your back, of course.

FLEX YOUR IDIOM MUSCLES

Verschlägt es einem **den** *Atem, hat man ein Dach über* **dem** *Kopf oder zermartert man sich* **das** *Gehirn, so drückt man dies im Deutschen gewöhnlich mit dem bestimmten Artikel (der, die, das) aus, im Englischen hingegen muss für solche Bezüge auf Teile des menschlichen Körpers meist ein Possessivpronomen (my/ your/his/her/its/our/your/their; Infinitiv: one's/someone's) – sowie gegebenenfalls der Plural – verwendet werden: It took* **my** *breath away; He needs a roof over* **his** *head; We were racking* **our** *brains.*

den Atem anhalten – hold one's breath

den Atem verschlagen – take one's breath away

etwas im Auge haben – have something in one's sights

vor etwas die Augen verschließen – close one's eyes to something

jemandem die Augen öffnen – open someone's eyes

wieder auf die Beine kommen – get back on one's feet

etwas im Blut haben – have something in one's blood

die Daumen drücken – keep one's fingers crossed

Däumchen drehen – twiddle one's thumbs

jemandem dicht auf den Fersen sein – be hot / hard on someone's heels

sich die Finger verbrennen – burn one's fingers / get one's fingers burned

jmdn. um den kleinen Finger wickeln – twist / wrap someone around one's little finger

jmdn. unter seine Fittiche nehmen – take someone under one's wing

jmdm. die Flügel stutzen – clip someone's wings

auf eigenen Füßen stehen – stand on one's own (two) feet

(immer wieder) auf die Füße fallen – land / fall on one's feet

sich das Gehirn zermartern – rack one's brains

Es steht ihm ins Gesicht geschrieben – It's written all over his face

jmdm. etwas ins Gesicht sagen – say sth to someone's face

ein Frosch im Hals – a frog in one's throat

sich die Hände reiben – rub one's hands

mit bloßen Händen – with one's bare hands

alle Hände voll zu tun haben – have one's hands full

jmdm. unter die Haut gehen	– get under someone's skin
am Herzen liegen	– be close to one's heart / be dear to one's heart
das Herz brechen	– break one's heart
ein Dach über dem Kopf	– a roof over one's head
den Kopf schütteln	– shake one's head
den Kopf verlieren	– lose one's head
jemandem seinen Kopf lassen	– give someone their head
jemandem zu Kopf steigen	– go to someone's head
jemandem den Kopf abreißen	– bite/snap someone's head off
jemanden in die Knie zwingen	– bring someone to their knees
jemandem Worte in den Mund legen	– put words into someone's mouth
die Muskeln spielen lassen	– flex one's muscles
jemandem im Nacken sitzen	– breathe down someone's neck
die Nase über jemanden / etwas rümpfen	– look down one's nose at something / someone
jemandem auf die Nerven gehen	– get on someone's nerves
die Ohren spitzen	– prick up one's ears
bis über die Ohren	– up to one's ears
jemandem / etwas den Rücken kehren	– turn one's back on someone / something
mit dem Rücken zur Wand	– with one's back to the wall
in den Schoß fallen	– fall / drop into one's lap
die Zähne zusammenbeißen	– grit one's teeth
jemandem auf die Zehen treten	– step on someone's toes
es liegt mir auf der Zunge	– it's on the tip of my tongue
sich auf die Zunge beißen	– bite one's tongue

ÜBERSETZUNG • BITTE ACHTEN SIE AUF DIE POSSESSIVPRONOMEN: MY, YOUR, HIS, HER . . .

1. Wir drücken Ihnen die Daumen.

2. Claudias Schönheit verschlug ihm den Atem.

3. Dieser Film ging mir wirklich unter die Haut.

4. Bitte lege mir keine Worte in den Mund.

5. Die Streiks haben das Land in die Knie gezwungen.

6. Wir haben zur Zeit alle Hände voll zu tun.

7. Du kannst vor diesem Problem nicht die Augen verschließen.

8. Unser Sohn steht jetzt auf eigenen Füßen.

9. Plötzlich hatte ich einen Frosch im Hals.

10. Ein kleiner Fehler und der Chef reißt dir den Kopf ab.

11. Ihre Freude steht ihr ins Gesicht geschrieben.

12. Das Glück meiner Frau liegt mir sehr am Herzen.

13. Ich kehrte Europa den Rücken und ging nach Amerika.

14. Unsere Firma ist bis über beide Ohren verschuldet.

15. Maggie wickelt all Männer um den kleinen Finger.

16. Dieser Pianist hat die Musik im Blut.

17. Während des Golfkriegs hielt die Welt den Atem an.

18. Ich sitze nur hier und drehe Däumchen.

19. Der Job ist ihm einfach in den Schoß gefallen.

20. Sein Reichtum ist ihm zu Kopf gestiegen.

21. Wir müssen jetzt die Zähne zusammenbeißen und weitermachen.

22. Tom's Arroganz geht mir auf die Nerven.

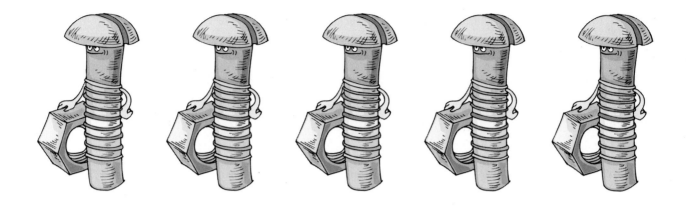

IDIOMS: THE NUTS AND BOLTS OF ENGLISH

*L*ike 'nuts and bolts' there are many fixed idiomatic phrases linked by 'and'. They are always used in a certain fixed order, e.g. 'nuts and bolts', never 'bolts and nuts'. Pair up the elements in the grey box by combining them with 'and', forming expressions that complete the sentences below.

dribs	milk	peace		blood	ends	parcel
flesh	nuts	pros	*and*	bolts	honey	quiet
law	odds	rules		cons	limb	regulations
life	part	wear		drabs	order	tear

1. The problem with Tom is that he never finishes a job properly but does everything in _____ .

2. For my next holiday I'll hire a small cottage in the woods and just enjoy the _____ .

3. I know my brother is impossible, but I've got to help him, after all he's my own _____ .

4. If you are soft on criminals, you only encourage them, I believe in _____ .

5. Those firemen risked _____ when they rescued the people from the burning house.

6. Fred worked his way up from the shop floor and knows all the _____ of the business.

7. We've moved the larger pieces of furniture but there are a lot of _____ left.

8. Staying at a different hotel each night is all _____ of the life of a travelling salesman.

9. Let's not be too hasty, let's weigh the _____ carefully before we make a decision.

10. We have very strict _____ on safety.

11. A taxi must be designed to stand the constant _____ of daily use.

12. Everybody wanted a house in Brighton. It was a time of _____ for the local estate agents.

NEST EGG & PENNYWISE
FINANCIAL ADVISERS

My advice is: Don't put all your eggs in one basket

PUT YOUR IDIOM HOUSE IN ORDER

Sehr viel häufiger als das Deutsche verwendet das Englische „Allerweltsverben" wie **put, get, give, take**, die auch für eine Vielzahl von idiomatischen Ausdrücken herangezogen werden. Vergleichen Sie unter diesem Aspekt auch die deutschen Entsprechungen der folgenden Idioms.

put all one's eggs in one basket _____

put two and two together _____

put on ice _____

put out feelers _____

put someone in the picture _____

put someone/sth in the shade _____

put words into someone's mouth _____

put one's foot down _____

put the finishing touches to something _____

put the lid on something _____

NOW USE THESE IDIOMS TO COMPLETE THE SENTENCES.

1. Before resigning from a job you should _____ to see where you can get a better one.

2. A good teacher must be able to _____ her/his _____ , if necessary.

3. Martin is the best student in his year group and _____ everyone else _____ .

4. The whole trip was bad, but what _____ it was the cancellation of our return flight.

5. I'll complete my essay tonight, I just have to _____ it.

6. When the suspect started contradicting himself the police _____ and arrested him.

7. In buying shares on the stock market you should never _____ .

8. We can't act until we have the new figures, so let's _____ the project _____ until then.

9. I never said you were a snob, please don't _____ .

10. Before you accept the job let us _____ you _____ and explain what it entails.

A BIT OF GIVE AND TAKE

WRITE THE GERMAN EQUIVALENTS NEXT TO THE FOLLOWING IDIOMS.

give someone the cold shoulder _____

give someone an even break _____

give the green light _____

give someone a wide berth _____

give someone their head _____

give someone a piece of one's mind _____

give someone a dose of their own medicine _____

take to one's heels _____

take someone's breath away _____

take something to heart _____

take one's hat off to someone _____

take someone under your wing _____

take the plunge _____

take the words out of someone's mouth _____

NOW USE THESE IDIOMS TO COMPLETE THE SENTENCES.

1. I agree totally with what you say; you _____ .

2. You can't let people get away with everything, sometimes you have to _____ .

3. Max _____ his colleagues' advice _____ and his work has greatly improved.

4. Last year I decided to _____ and gave up my job to start my own business.

5. Parents should know when to say no and not just _____ children _____ .

6. When Austria's populist Haider came to power, European diplomats _____ .

7. The Clark family are noisy and abusive and neighbours _____ .

8. When the escaped bull started to run towards us, we _____ .

9. The teacher told the pupils she would _____ everybody _____ regardless of past results.

10. The film crew cheered when Hollywood bosses _____ their project _____ .

11. I admire firemen and _____ to them for the way in which they risk their lives.

12. Tim is too young to move to London, but Aunt Mabel has promised to _____ .

13. Ben always keeps us waiting, so we'll _____ and be late too.

14. The tourist saw the Grand Canyon for the first time and its beauty _____ .

59

REVISION: MULTIPLE CHOICE

Choose the idiomatic expression that goes with the sentence.

1. If that's a genuine Rembrandt, I'll _____ .

   ○ eat a broom   ○ **eat my hat**   ○ shout it from the rooftops

2. We all think Mr Day doesn't know his job, but nobody dares to say so _____ .

   ○ to his face   ○ in his face   ○ face to face

3. Just tell me what you want and don't _____ .

   ○ call a spade a spade   ○ beat about the bush   ○ break the ice

4. We all thought he'd stay with our company forever, so his resignation came as _____ .

   ○ lightning out of a blue sky   ○ much ado about nothing   ○ a bolt from the blue

5. Their son's confession that he had stolen several cars _____ .

   ○ shook his parents to the core   ○ was music to his parents' ears   ○ killed two birds with one stone

6. Alan easily loses his temper, and he's in a terrible mood today. One wrong word and he _____ .

   ○ walks a tightrope   ○ spills the beans   ○ flies off the handle

7. Hey John, the value of our shares has gone up again. – Great! That's _____ .

   ○ music to my ears   ○ music for my ears   ○ a bright spark

8. To run a successful business you have to _____ with modern technology.

   ○ keep step   ○ keep pace   ○ push your luck

9. Adam had hoped that Lynn would accept his dinner invitation but she _____ .

    ○ gave him an even break   ○ took his breath away   ○ gave him the cold shoulder

10. Let's renovate one room after the other and not try to do the whole house at once. Let's not _____ .

    ○ go through the motions   ○ get the hang of it   ○ bite off more than we can chew

11. My niece is the most intelligent pupil in her year group, she really is a _____ .

    ○ bright head   ○ bright spark   ○ rough diamond

12. Our garage is _____ because Dad puts all the gardening tools in it.

    ○ bursting at the seams   ○ bursting out of the seams   ○ cracking at the seams

13. I don't understand a word he says. He's speaking _____ .

    ○ in puzzles   ○ in enigmas   ○ in riddles

14. We've just lost a big client and still have to repay a bank loan, so our finances are pretty much _____ .

    ○ on a roll   ○ at a low ebb   ○ off the hook

15. Our new nanny is great with the children. I think we've really _____ with her.

    ○ settled the score   ○ hit the jackpot   ○ picked a bone

16. This computer is quite easy to handle once you _____ .

    ○ rack your brains   ○ push your luck   ○ get the hang of it

17. I've worked non-stop for a month and I'm totally exhausted. I'm really _____ .

    ○ at the end of my tether   ○ on cloud nine   ○ on a roll

18. People say that faith can _____ .

    ○ replace mountains   ○ move mountains   ○ move a mountain

19. She promised to write to me but she never did; oh well I suppose it's a case of _____ .

    ○ out of sight, out of mind   ○ let sleeping dogs lie   ○ still waters run deep

20. You can trust Harry. He's _____ and has got a lot of experience.

    ○ an old hare   ○ an old master   ○ an old hand

21. Mr Fogey is the president of the company, but it is the managing director who _____ .

    ○ calls the tune   ○ does the trick   ○ beats about the bush

I went to London with my car.

REVISION: SPOT THE MISTAKE

1. I went to London ~~with~~ my car. _____ **Correct: I went to London in my car / by car.** _____

2. You must not lose the head now. _____

3. My job is hanging on a thread. _____

4. I never said that! Please don't lay words into my mouth. _____

5. I'm tired of having to play the second fiddle all the time. _____

6. The leader of a parliamentary fraction in the House of Commons is called 'The Whip'. _____

7. The number of nature catastrophes has grown in recent years. _____

8. It's very hard to find a park space in European cities these days. _____

9. I'm off to lunch, can you hold the position for me in the meantime? _____

10. The investment adviser promised me golden mountains, but I didn't believe him. _____

11. Her sudden resignation was like lightning from a blue sky. _____

12. I'd like to apologise by you for my behaviour yesterday. _____

13. This elegant finely crafted ring is made of massive gold. _____

14. 'Hello, Mike. Great to see you,' he shouted at me, waving and smiling. _____

15. I know Pete's made a mistake but to call him totally incompetent was a blow under the belt. _____

REVISION: TRANSLATION

1. Kopf hoch! Wir drücken Ihnen die Daumen.

2. Wenn alle Stricke reißen, können wir ja ein Taxi nehmen.

3. Wie wär's mit einem Bier?

4. Sarah redet viel, aber in Anne hat sie ihren Meister gefunden.

5. Kennst du die Öffnungszeiten der Handelskammer?

6. Er zeigte uns die kalte Schulter und rührte keinen Finger, um uns zu helfen.

7. Der Tower ist Teil unseres Kulturerbes.

8. Nach allem, was ich weiß, kann man in Ashford nach Canterbury umsteigen.

9. Also, eigentlich würde ich lieber zu Hause bleiben.

10. Mit dieser Bemerkung zeigte er sein wahres Gesicht.

11. Mit meinem neuen Job habe ich wirklich das große Los gezogen.

12. Ich habe Grundkenntnisse in Gentechnologie.

13. In 1992 wurde in einem amerikanischen Wohngebiet Giftmüll entdeckt.

14. Das habe ich nur aus Spaß gesagt.